Chemical and Biological Warfare

The Cruelest Weapons

Chemical and Biological Warfare

The Cruelest Weapons

Laurence Pringle

— Issues in Focus—

ENSLOW PUBLISHERS, INC.

Bloy St. and Ramsey Ave.   P.O. Box 38
Box 777   Aldershot
Hillside, N.J. 07205   Hants GU12 6BP
U.S.A.   U.K.

Library of Congress Cataloging-in-Publication Data

Pringle, Laurence P.
    Chemical and biological warfare: the cruelest weapons/Laurence Pringle.
       p.cm.—(Issues in focus)
    Includes bibliographical references and index.
    ISBN 0-89490-280-6
    1. Chemical warfare. 2. Biological warfare. I. Title.
  II. Series: Issues in focus (Hillside, N.J.)
    UG447.P758   1993
    358'.34—dc20

                         92-16641
                         CIP

Printed in the United States of America

10 9 8 7 6 5 4 3 2 1

Illustration Credits:
AP/Wide World Photos, pp. 11, 43, 56, 58; Bureau of Land Management,
p. 35; Department of Defense, pp. 46, 61, 63, 86; Dr. Joan Nowicki,
Smithsonian Institution, p. 51; General Dynamics, p. 62; Harriet Goitein,
p. 65; The Metropolitan Museum of Art, Gift of J. Pierpont Morgan, 1917,
p. 15; National Archives, pp. 8, 19, 21, 23, 27, 30, 40; United Nations
Photo 158591/ H. Ardvisson, p. 66; United Nations Photo 168765/Milton
Grant, p. 84; U.S. Army, pp. 80, 82; U.S. Department of Agriculture, p.
75; World Health Organization Photo, p. 33.
Cover Illustration:
Chip Hires / Gamma-Liaison Network

Contents

Acknowledgements

The author thanks Gordon Burck, Senior Policy Analyst, EAI Corporation; and Mathew Meselson, Professor of Bio-Chemistry and Molecular Biology, Harvard University, for reading the manuscript of this book and helping to improve its accuracy.

Poison gases were a major, widely-used weapon just once in history, during World War I.

1

"Mysterious, Devilish Thing"

In the 1935–1936 war between Italy and Ethiopia, the Ethiopians feared but understood artillery shells and bombs from aircraft. Then the Italian air force began dropping drums and bombs of poisonous gas and spraying a deadly rain of chemicals from low-flying airplanes. Ethiopia was defeated, partly because these chemical arms caused low morale among civilians and soldiers. A British observer wrote that poison gas was something outside the Ethiopians' experience, "a mysterious, devilish thing."

Both chemical and biological weapons can be called mysterious, devilish things. Although exploding bombs, missiles, and artillery shells have caused much more death and destruction, clouds of toxic chemicals and the invisible deadliness of "germ" warfare frighten people almost as much as the ultimate horror: nuclear war.

9

Nuclear, chemical, and biological weapons have some similar qualities that frighten people. They are unfamiliar hazards that seem capable of killing or injuring many people at once. They also seem uncontrollable. Biological and some chemical weapons are invisible, as is nuclear radiation. These characteristics, and the fact that chemical and biological weapons are almost always used against defenseless populations, cause people to dread them.

According to a 1969 United Nations report, chemical weapons are "chemical substances, whether gaseous, liquid, or solid, which might be employed because of their direct toxic effects on man, animals, and plants." Biological weapons are "living organisms, whatever their nature, or infective material derived from them, which are intended to cause disease or death in man, animals, or plants, and which depend for their effects on their ability to multiply in the person, animal, or plant attacked."

Since 1925 more than 100 nations have signed an agreement called the Geneva Protocol, barring the first use of chemical and biological weapons in war. Several nations have since ignored this accord. During the 1980s, for example, Iraq released poisonous gases against Iranian troops. Again in 1988 Iraq used chemical weapons to put down a rebellion of its own Kurdish citizens.

One outcome of the 1991 Persian Gulf War was that Iraq agreed to give up all materials and equipment for making chemical and biological weapons. Nevertheless, according to former Central Intelligence Agency (CIA)

10

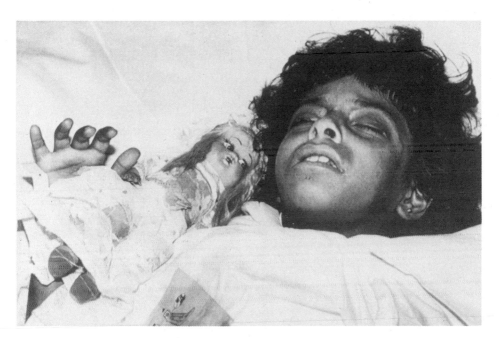

This Kurdish girl was one of the many people injured in 1988 when Iraq used chemical weapons on its own people. She was a victim of mustard gas poisoning.

director William Webster, nearly twenty other nations have the chemical industry that enables them to make such weapons. In fact, some countries already have stockpiles of such arms.

"Destroy them," urge the United States and other nations that have huge arsenals of conventional arms as well as nuclear weapons. To countries lacking conventional and nuclear arms, however, chemical and biological weapons have a special appeal. In the Middle East, for example, several Arab nations believe that they must have the option to make chemical weapons to counter the chemical and nuclear arms of Israel. Chemical and biological weapons are seen as a sort of "equalizer." Cheaper and easier to produce than nuclear weapons, they have been called "the poor man's atomic bomb."

Nasty as they are, chemical and biological weapons pose a limited threat in warfare—so far. But genetic engineering may enable scientists to create from living organisms more deadly varieties of diseases. These weapons could be more dangerous, more cruel, than those already in existence.

This book explores all of these matters, and concludes with the great challenge facing earth's community of nations: to halt the production of chemical and biological weapons and to keep them from becoming an even greater menace to humankind.

2

From Smoke Screens to Mustard Gas

People wonder: When were chemical or biological weapons first used in war? The answer may be before recorded history. Perhaps the first chemical weapon was smoke. Armies burned freshly-cut wood and leaves in order to create smoke to conceal their advance, to force their opponents out of hiding, or even to suffocate their enemies in cave hideouts.

Beginning at least 3,000 years ago, soldiers added chemicals to fires in order to produce fumes that choked or sickened enemies. Weapons based on fire were used in the Peloponnesian War, a conflict between different states in Greece that began in 432 B.C. Armies laid siege to walled cities. A primitive flamethrower—fire propelled by bellows through a giant pipe—burned the wooden walls of one town. Defenders of the Greek city Syracuse made a highly flammable mixture of pitch, sulfur, pine sawdust, and other ingredients to destroy the Athenian battering rams that attacked their walls.

"Greek fire" was a chemical weapon, perhaps invented in A.D. 660 by a Greek engineer named Callinicus. It helped Byzantine Greeks repulse several attacks by Arabs and Russians on the port city of Constantinople. In 673, for example, a Saracen (Arab) fleet was nearly destroyed by jets of liquid fire emitted from tubes that protruded from Greek galleys. Water tossed on the flames only caused the fire to burn more fiercely.

The original "recipe" of Greek fire is not known. It probably included pitch, sulfur, quicklime, and naphtha—the Greek term for the petroleum that they collected from surface pools.

Biological warfare—using disease as a weapon—developed more recently than chemical warfare. Scientists did not prove that "germs" (bacteria, viruses, and rickettsia) cause infectious diseases until the nineteenth century. Long before then, however, people observed that some diseases seemed to be spread by contact with a sick or dead person, or by drinking water contaminated with the decaying body of an animal. That knowledge was put to use in warfare; for example, throwing human corpses or animal carcasses down wells to poison an enemy population's water supply.

An early instance of biological warfare that was recorded in detail occurred in 1346. Tartars had laid

Fiery chemical weapons were developed both to defend and attack walled cities and castles. This siege scene was carved in a medieval ivory casket lid.

siege to the port city of Caffa (now Feodosya in the Ukraine) on the east coast of the Black Sea. Caffa was inhabited mostly by Italian merchants and soldiers, who showed no signs of weakening. Then a deadly infectious disease, the plague, struck the Tartars; thousands died. According to Italian historian Gabriel de Mussis, the Tartars turned their disease victims into weapons:

> The Tartars, fatigued by such a plague and pestiferous disease, stupefied and amazed, observing themselves dying without hope of health, ordered cadavers placed on their hurling machine and thrown into the city of Caffa, so that by means of these intolerable passengers the defenders died widely. Thus there were projected mountains of dead, nor could the Christians hide or flee, or be freed from such disaster. . . . And soon all the air was infected and the water poisoned, corrupt and putrified.

The Italians gave up the city. Then fleeing to Italy by sea, the survivors unwittingly helped spread the deadly plague to Europe.

Biological warfare also helped European invaders defeat the natives of North America. During the French and Indian War, the commander-in-chief of the British forces urged that smallpox be spread to the Indians. "You will do well to try to inoculate the Indians by means of blankets," he wrote to the commander of Fort Pitt, which was located where the city of Pittsburgh, Pennsylvania, now stands. In 1763 a British captain met with two Indian chiefs and gave them gifts of blankets that had been brought from a smallpox hospital. According to historians, smallpox soon raged among the tribes of the region.

Overall, however, chemical weapons have been further developed and more frequently used than biological weapons. The British fired artillery shells loaded with picric acid during the Boer War (1899–1902) in southern Africa. The resulting fumes were not, however, an effective weapon.

Chlorine gas was proposed as a weapon for the Union forces during the Civil War in the United States. But Edwin Stanton, secretary of war, rejected a plan to fire chlorine-filled shells at Confederate troops. Some fifty years later, however, chlorine *was* used in modern warfare—with horrifying results that turned world opinion against chemical weapons.

In 1915 World War I was a stalemate, with opposing forces dug into trenches. Both sides had fired tear gas shells in unsuccessful efforts to dislodge their opponents. Near the Belgian city of Ypres, German forces were faced by French and Algerian troops. In the late afternoon of April 22, the wind was blowing toward the Allied trenches. German troops released 168 tons of liquid chlorine from nearly 6,000 cylinders that they had hauled to the front lines under cover of darkness.

A yellow cloud of poisonous gas drifted across no-man's-land to the Allied lines. Heavier than air, the chlorine gas settled into the trenches and deep shelters where the Allied troops thought they were safe.

Chlorine gas irritates the eyes, nose, and throat. It blinded some soldiers, while causing many others to choke to death. Trying to escape the gas attack, still other soldiers ran in panic, deeply inhaled the chlorine, and also died. The attack killed an estimated 5,000 men and wounded another 10,000. It opened a four-mile-wide breach in the Allied front lines. The Germans had not expected such success, however, and did not have enough troops poised to exploit this opportunity.

Two days later German troops released more chlorine gas. This time the victims were Canadian troops, who had been given cloth, to be dipped in urine or bicarbonate of soda, for use as a primitive gas mask. Many died, but the Canadian forces were able to fend off attacking German troops. From April 1915 until the war's end in 1918, both sides rushed to develop and use poison gases and the defenses against them.

In late September 1915 British troops launched a chlorine gas attack on German positions in Belgium. It was a success, leading to the capture of more than 3,000 German soldiers. However, it also illustrated a limitation and danger of chemical warfare that affects military thinking to this day. The wind had shifted and carried chlorine toward the British lines, causing casualties and an abrupt end to the gas attack. Over a three-week period,

Canadian troops charge from a trench in World War I. In order
to break the stalemate of trench warfare, Germany launched poison
gas attacks.

some 2,400 British men were injured by poison gas released from their own lines.

Poison gas attacks became a basic part of the war. Both sides fired artillery and mortar shells loaded with deadly chemicals. World War I became a chemical warfare test, with as many as fifty different types of gas used on the experimental animals—humans. By late 1915 the Germans were using phosgene, an almost invisible gas that causes victims to choke, gasp for air, and suffocate. It smells like new-mown hay, but is ten times as deadly as chlorine. Within months the British were also launching phosgene attacks.

Troops on both sides, and even cavalry horses and mules, now wore improved gas masks. Gas attacks, consequently, became less effective. Sometimes, to overcome this defense, two gases were released together. The Germans mixed chloropicrin, which penetrated masks well, with phosgene. Chloropicrin caused nausea and vomiting. When the soldiers raised their gas masks to throw up, they would inhale the deadly phosgene.

In July 1917 Germany took the lead in the chemical arms race. German soldiers attacked—again near Ypres, Belgium—with a new gas delivered in artillery shells. The new and more deadly weapon was dichloroethyl sulfide, known simply as mustard gas or just mustard. In concentrated form it has a sharp smell like mustard or horseradish.

Bursting shells spewed out an oily brown liquid and

By late 1915, troops on both sides wore gas masks, and so did their horses and mules.

an acrid gas. At first the substances seemed harmless. Many Allied soldiers removed their masks. Within a few hours, however, mustard gas began to cause vomiting, severe burns, and temporary blindness. Gas masks were effective at preventing internal injuries, but the gas could seep into boots and penetrate several layers of cloth, causing huge blisters.

Within three weeks, German mustard gas attacks had caused 15,000 British casualties. Mustard became known as the "king of the war gases," partly because it persisted in liquid form for days after being released. The Germans used it for defensive purposes, trying to create mustard-splattered zones to block the forward movement of Allied forces.

Near the war's end Allied forces were also attacking with mustard gas. One casualty was a young Bavarian courier named Adolph Hitler, who later wrote, in *Mein Kampf,* of his experience of being temporarily blinded. By 1918 artillery barrages often included as many gas shells as high-explosive shells. Altogether, 113,000 tons of poison gases were used in World War I. Chemical warfare caused an estimated 92,000 deaths and 1.3 million total casualties. Total casualties during World War I were 21 million and, military historians agree, chemical arms did not have a decisive effect on the outcome of the war.

Their use did, however, have other effects. One was global revulsion toward chemical warfare. The end of

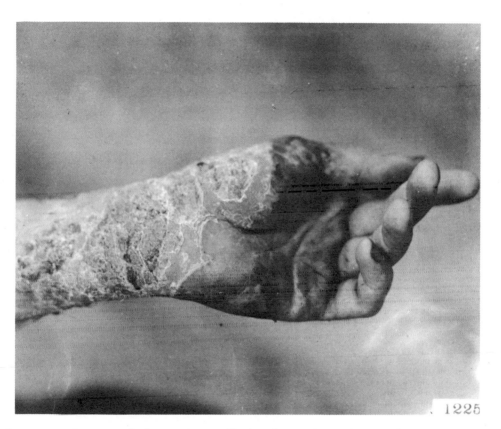

1225

As gas masks became more effective the warring nations tried new types of gases, including mustard, which causes the wound shown.

World War I marked the beginning of an effort in the League of Nations to outlaw chemical weapons. The result was the 1925 Geneva Protocol. (Its full name is "Protocol for the prohibition of the use in war of asphyxiating, poisonous or other gases, and of bacteriological methods of warfare.") Some 130 nations (including Iraq) have signed this accord. Although it has discouraged the use of chemical weapons, it has several loopholes.

One loophole is that the protocol has no provision for punishing nations that use chemical or biological weapons. Another is that it does not prohibit making and storing such arms or threatening to use them. A third flaw is the protocol's vagueness about what it prohibits. Should "other gases" include tear gases, or the herbicides that the United States rained down on Vietnam? In 1969 eighty-nine countries in the United Nations voted in favor of including such "nonlethal" weapons, but their vote was only a recommendation, not binding on parties of the Geneva Protocol.

Many survivors of World War I poison gas attacks lived with horrible memories of that moment when the toxic clouds billowed toward them or when mustard blistered their skin. Many suffered chronic illness, scarred lungs, or an early death. For these survivors, and for the dead, the first attempt to outlaw chemical and biological weapons came too late to help.

3

Nerve Gases and Germ Warfare

The United States first sent troops to Europe in June 1917. Yet a quarter of its casualties—70,000 men—were victims of gas attacks. At military facilities in Maryland, the United States began producing great quantities of its own chemical weapons. The war ended, however, before they were put to use.

Between 1935 and 1936, as mentioned, the Italian air force sprayed mustard from airplanes flying over Ethiopia. It also dropped bombs that exploded 200 feet above the ground, releasing a mist of mustard on Ethiopian soldiers and civilians. Between 1937 and 1945, Japan, too, used poison gases against unprotected peasants and soldiers during its invasion and occupation of China. The Japanese also engaged in biological warfare. This was the first documented case of germ warfare since the British attempt to spread smallpox among Native Americans 174 years earlier.

An estimated 3,000 Chinese, Korean, Russian, American, and other prisoners died in experiments as Japanese scientists studied the effectiveness of several diseases. Bombs containing bacteria as well as wads of cotton containing other disease agents were dropped on eleven Chinese cities. Among the germ warfare weapons was the plague, which killed hundreds of Chinese.

Japan's biological and chemical attacks in China were also the only use of such weapons during World War II. This fact is remarkable. Both sides battling for control of Europe had stockpiles of deadly chemicals. Clearly, the potential for all-out chemical and biological war was there, but both sides feared retaliation.

Germany, in particular, had developed new chemical arms that could have killed many thousands of Allied troops. German scientists had discovered that chemicals related to insecticides, called tabun, sarin, and soman, were also nerve gases. Tabun was the first nerve gas and one that Germany produced in great amounts during World War II. (The others, developed a few years later, were even more deadly.)

Colorless and odorless, nerve gases can be inhaled or absorbed through the skin. Within the body they block the action of an enzyme that serves to end transmission of nerve impulses. The result is wild, uncontrollable nerve signals to muscles, including those that control

Chemical weapons caused a quarter of all United States' casualties in World War I.

breathing. Victims lose control of their bodies. Violent convulsions are soon followed by suffocation.

Nazi Germany had more than 12,000 tons of one such gas stockpiled by 1945. Historians have speculated about why none of these horrible weapons were used. One factor, perhaps, was Adolph Hitler's own personal experience with gas warfare in World War I. More important, Germany's military commanders believed that the United States and other Allied powers had nerve gases, too, and feared retaliation. Also, late in the war when Germany might have taken desperate steps to turn the tide of battle, its air force was too weak to deliver a major nerve gas attack.

Germany's information about the Allies having nerve gases was wrong. Both the United States and Great Britain did, however, have great quantities of mustard and other chemical weapons. In 1944 the Prime Minister of Great Britain, Winston Churchill, urged his commanders to study the possibility of "drenching" German cities with toxic gases. This chemical warfare was never carried out; nor did Great Britain use the biological weapons it had begun to produce in the late 1930s.

In the United States, research on biological weapons began in 1942 at a Maryland army camp, now called Fort Detrick. Scientists began studying ways to make weapons of such diseases as typhus, cholera, yellow fever, plague, anthrax, and botulism. The last two initially received the most attention. Both anthrax and botulism originate with bacteria; both strike quickly, and can be deadly.

Aided by the British, the United States developed the first biological bomb in 1943. It weighed four pounds and contained anthrax spores. Soon U.S. scientists had also made bombs containing botulism toxin, a deadly poison that people sometimes consume in food. Had the United States chosen to do so, it had the capacity to make many thousands of anthrax or botulism bombs each month.

Near the end of the war in Europe, U.S. scientists were also trying to make a weapon of brucellosis, or undulant fever. Caused by a bacterium, undulant fever is seldom fatal, but can make people ill for months. The United States also had developed several chemicals for use against plants, specifically, against rice crops in Japan.

Plans for destroying Japan's rice crop from the air were still under study in the summer of 1945. They were never put in action. Instead, another kind of new weapon, the atomic bomb, was dropped on two Japanese cities. Japan surrendered in mid-August, 1945.

Soon after the end of World War II, the United States was engaged in another, different kind of war—the so-called Cold War of hostile, suspicious relations between the western powers and the communist-run Soviet Union and its allies. The Soviets had captured a nerve gas factory in eastern Germany, disassembled it,

Opposing nations in World War II had stocks of chemical arms but
did not use them.

and had it reassembled in Russia. In Japan, the United States also scored a coup: It captured the leaders of Japan's biological warfare program.

In 1949 the Soviet Union accused the United States of protecting the leaders of Japan's inhumane germ warfare research on American and other prisoners of war. The United States dismissed the charge as "propaganda." But documents released in following years show that the accusation was accurate; a deal had been made. Japanese researchers, even though they had probably committed war crimes, were not prosecuted. In return the United States obtained details of the only known research on the effects of biological weapons on human subjects. By avoiding a war crimes trial, the United States was able to keep this information secret.

Fear of communism fueled U.S. research on chemical and biological weapons. In 1960 the head of U.S. army research claimed that a massive effort to produce chemical arms was underway in the Soviet Union. The U.S. budget for research and development of such weapons soared. It grew from about $10 million a year in the early 1950s to $352 million in 1969. (Many of these funds were spent on tear gas and herbicides used in the Vietnam War.) Some researchers worked for the military at Fort Detrick and other facilities; others worked for some 300 private companies, research institutes, and universities.

A variety of chemical and biological weapons were

developed. They included nerve gases that could be released from land mines, and saxitoxin, a deadly shellfish poison, placed on the tips of scores of bullet-size darts that exploded in all directions from a 500-pound cluster bomb. At Fort Detrick scientists learned how to raise a half million *Aedes aegypti* mosquitoes a month and infect them with yellow fever. They planned, but never built, a plant that each month could have reared 130 million of these disease-carrying mosquitoes.

Most of the research on biological weapons was a well-kept secret until the 1970s, when many government documents were released as a result of the Freedom of Information Act. It was not until 1977 or later that the public learned that many people had served as guinea pigs, beginning in 1951. (These tests are described in detail in Leonard Cole's *Clouds of Secrecy: The Army's Germ Warfare Tests over Populated Areas.*)

In order to learn how to detect biological warfare agents, and also to find the most effective ways to spread them among a population, the U.S. military decided to conduct secret open-air tests using live microorganisms. Some of this research was conducted far from population centers; for example, at the Dugway Proving Ground in Utah. Some was conducted in major U.S. cities.

In 1955 the Central Intelligence Agency (CIA) obtained supplies of whooping cough bacteria from Fort Detrick, and then conducted studies along the Gulf Coast of Florida. According to Florida's medical records,

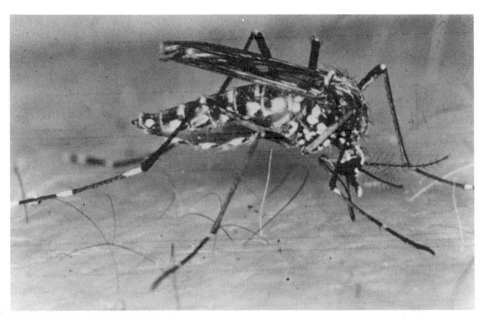

The *Aedes aegypti* mosquito carries yellow fever, and could be raised in huge numbers to be released as a biological weapon.

the number of cases of whooping cough tripled that year. There were 339 cases and one death in 1954; 1,080 cases and 12 deaths in 1955. The CIA also conducted tests of mind-altering drugs on hundreds of people without their knowledge.

As a general rule, however, military researchers used what they called biological simulants in their tests on unsuspecting people. These were bacteria or other microorganisms that "behaved" like disease-causing organisms, but which were believed to be harmless. For example, to simulate a biological warfare attack in the United States, scientists used bacteria called *Bacillus subtilis.* It has many of the characteristics of *Bacillus anthracis,* which causes anthrax. Defending use of this simulant in 1977, army researchers said that there was no evidence that it was harmful to people. Nevertheless, there were warnings in the medical reference books that *subtilis* did sometimes cause infections.

This sort of research went on for two decades, 1949–1969. Millions of people were exposed to several varieties of bacteria released in more than 230 populated areas. The test sites included Minneapolis, St. Louis, Washington, D.C., and the New York City subway system. Army researchers made no attempt to monitor the health of target populations. When the secret tests were finally revealed, during U.S. Senate hearings in 1977, army spokesmen continued to argue that the simulant organisms were harmless. Doctors who testified disagreed.

An accidental release of nerve gas killed herds of sheep in Utah. This 1968 incident drew attention to U.S. research on chemical and biological weapons.

They said that exposure to heavy concentrations of even "harmless" bacteria can cause illness and that the secret tests had been a health hazard.

An incident in 1968 drew the attention of news media and the public to the U.S. biological and chemical weapons research. VX nerve gas was being released from a jet aircraft flying low over a target area at Dugway Proving Ground, Utah. As the jet climbed to a higher altitude, about twenty pounds of the nerve gas was accidentally dispersed. Winds carried the VX gas eastward more than thirty-five miles, to an area where sheep grazed. Six thousand sheep died or had to be destroyed because of possible contamination.

The government denied responsibility for several months, which only intensified questioning from news media and the public. Finally, army researchers admitted the accident. The victims were sheep, not people, but this mistaken release of nerve gas fueled opposition to research on chemical and biological weapons.

4

Agent Orange and Yellow Rain

In the late 1960s the United States had a large arsenal of chemical and biological weapons, but opposition to the program grew in Congress. The Vietnam War was an underlying cause for this change. As the war dragged on, more and more people questioned the tactics of the United States's forces and even their presence in Southeast Asia. American use of chemical weapons helped erode public confidence in the United States' involvement.

The weapons were types of tear gas and herbicides (plant-killing chemicals). The United States contended that these chemicals were not the sort prohibited by the Geneva Protocol. However, the ways in which massive amounts of these compounds were used led many scientists and other people to oppose this kind of warfare.

Use of chemical weapons began on a small scale in

1962, when the United States supplied the South Vietnamese Army with riot control gases (sometimes called tear gases, irritant agents, or harassing agents). The most common was called CS. By 1965 U.S. troops were using CS to force enemy soldiers from their networks of underground tunnels and bunkers. (In a confined space, CS and other tear gases do not easily disperse and can be as lethal as other chemical weapons.)

Eventually CS was also used for defensive purposes; for example, in booby traps around the perimeter of a camp. As an offensive weapon, CS was released in 55-gallon drums from helicopters. Just before a B-52 bomb attack or a sweep by ground forces, vast amounts of CS were dispersed over forested areas, in hopes of driving the Viet Cong out into the open.

Some 13.7 million pounds of CS were used in the Vietnam War. Between 1962 and 1971 the United States also drenched Vietnam and parts of neighboring Laos with nearly nineteen million gallons of herbicides. They were called Agents Blue, White, Purple, and Orange. Agents Purple and Orange were a mixture of two plant-killing chemicals that in 1970 were banned in the United States because they were judged to be hazardous to human health.

President John F. Kennedy had approved use of these herbicides in late November 1961. The chemical-spraying program, called Operation Ranch Hand, was aimed at destroying crops (to deny the enemy food) and to defoliate trees (to deny the enemy cover). Agent Blue killed rice plants, while Agent White slowly killed trees. Agents Purple and Orange quickly killed the leaves of trees and shrubs.

Between 1962 and 1971 Operation Ranch Hand sprayed nearly six million acres of South Vietnam. Almost 90 percent of the herbicides were used to defoliate forests. Wide swaths were sprayed alongside roads and railroads in an attempt to reduce the threat of ambushes. Herbicides also rained down around base camps (to aid their defense) and on forests (where enemy camps or infiltration routes were hidden).

Although the U.S. military continued to support this program, some military experts questioned its value. Defoliation may have actually improved the field of fire for ambushers, and removed cover in which ambushed troops could hide. The sharpest criticism, however, was aimed at crop spraying.

Interviews with civilians and former Viet Cong soldiers showed that crop spraying did not cause any serious food shortages for enemy troops. The crop destruction did, however, cause hardship for many peasants and their families. It also increased their bitter feelings toward the United States and the South Vietnam government.

By the mid-1960s, scientists were increasingly concerned about herbicide use in Vietnam. They first worried about the long-term effects on forests and cropland, and later about the effects of dioxin—a highly toxic

The tear gas CS was used as an offensive weapon in the Vietnam War. Here, barrels of CS are dropped from a helicopter.

substance present in Agent Orange—on the health of civilians. (Eventually, thousands of U.S. Vietnam veterans claimed that they had impaired health from exposure to Agent Orange.) In early 1967 more than 5,000 U.S. scientists signed a petition that urged an end to the use of CS and plant-killing chemicals in Vietnam.

Their views joined countless others from both home and abroad. In 1969 the United Nations passed a resolution stating that the Geneva Protocol prohibited "any chemical agents of warfare . . . which might be employed because of their direct toxic effects on humans, animals, or plants." This was clearly aimed at United States' use of herbicides. Eighty-nine nations voted in favor of this resolution. Only the United States and two other countries voted against it, although thirty-six nations—mostly U.S. allies—abstained from voting.

Members of Congress threatened major cuts in funds for chemical and biological weapons. President Richard Nixon ordered a review of the U.S. program, and in November 1969 he announced major changes. The United States would stop making biological weapons and destroy its stocks of them. It would, however, continue to study defenses against such weapons. The United States would also give up first use of chemical arms, using them only in response to a chemical attack. (Many nations that have ratified the Geneva Protocol take the same position.)

The United States continued to claim that herbicides

and CS gases were not lethal weapons, and would still be used in Vietnam. Their use was phased out, however.

Public outrage and protests from scientists were not the only reasons for the dramatic change in U.S. policy. Another reason was the realization that development of biological weapons might, in the long run, harm U.S. interests. Biological weapons can be produced cheaply. According to a report to the United Nations in 1969 (using 1969 prices), in a large-scale military attack on civilians, "casualties might cost about $2,000 per square kilometer with conventional weapons, $800 with nuclear weapons, $600 with nerve gas weapons, and $1 with biological weapons."

Poor nations with biological arms would easily gain highly destructive weapons. This would change the world's balance of power. Matthew Meselson, an expert on such weapons and a professor of biochemistry at Harvard University, wrote in 1964, "The introduction of radically cheap weapons of mass destruction into the arsenals of the world would not act as much to strengthen the big powers as it would endow dozens of relatively weak countries with great destructive capacity."

Thus the United States had a strong incentive to discourage the spread of biological and chemical arms. It showed renewed interest in negotiating a new international agreement on this matter. The treaty, completed in 1971 and opened for ratification in 1972, is called the Biological Weapons Convention. The Biological

The United States sprayed nearly six million acres of South Vietnam with Agent Orange and other plant-killing chemicals.

Weapons Convention, which took effect in 1975, was a major step in disarmament. It prohibits development, production, and stockpiling of biological arms as well as their use. (This includes toxins, which are poisonous substances produced by bacteria and other living organisms.)

One hundred and eighteen nations have since agreed to its terms. The Biological Weapons Convention is stronger than the Geneva Protocol, but it too has troublesome loopholes. It lacks procedures for verifying complaints that a nation is breaking its rules. And the defensive research it allows—for example, developing vaccines and protective gear against germ warfare diseases—can have offensive uses as well.

In its introduction, the Biological Weapons Convention asserted that it was a first possible step toward a similar treaty prohibiting the development and stockpiling of chemical arms. The United States and the Soviet Union began to negotiate the terms of this treaty that became the Chemical Weapons Convention of 1993.

In 1972 the Chemical Corps of the U.S. Department of Defense was closed. Its stocks of biological weapons were destroyed and its production plants shut down. The Department of Defense budget for chemical and biological arms shrank to about $75 million, a modern low, in 1975.

The Department of Defense, and supporters of the Chemical Corps in Congress, began to emphasize a new way to deliver deadly chemicals, called binary munitions.

(Actually, U.S. research on these weapons has been traced back to 1949.) Binary weapons consist of two chemical compounds that mix and produce a nerve gas within an artillery shell or other munition while it is in flight. For battlefield troops, it was claimed, these weapons would be safer to use than other chemical arms. They would also be safer to store and transport, whether in battle or in peacetime near civilian populations.

Financial support for chemical warfare research began to rise dramatically in 1980, the year Ronald Reagan was elected President. Cold War tensions had grown in the late 1970s, and President Reagan held rigid anti-Soviet views. There was increased worry—or paranoia—that the Soviets were disregarding the Biological Weapons Convention and forging ahead with new and more deadly chemical and biological weapons.

Beginning in 1978, newspaper reports from Thailand told of Laotian refugees who claimed that their villages had been attacked with poison gases from communist aircraft. The U.S. State Department sent officers to interview some of the refugees, who said that the gases from exploding bombs or rockets, or sprayed from planes, caused vomiting, diarrhea, and sometimes death. Other symptoms were also reported. A U.S. Army medical team also interviewed some refugees. Its report was made public in December 1979. It concluded that two or three chemical weapons had been used, including a nerve

These soldiers are wearing field protective masks as they train in Quantico, Virginia in 1980. That year, chemical warfare research began to rise dramatically.

gas. It also claimed that perhaps as many as 1,000 Laotian refugees had died.

Rebels in Afghanistan also reported that Soviet troops had used chemical weapons. These reports, and those from Southeast Asia, fueled the Reagan Administration's belief that the Soviets could not be trusted to honor treaties. In September 1981 Secretary of State Alexander Haig claimed that the United States had physical evidence that the Soviet Union and its allies had used highly toxic poisons in Southeast Asia.

The U.S. State Department soon revealed its evidence. In addition to the interviews with refugees, there was a leaf and a stem covered with tiny yellow dots collected from Cambodia. The alleged poison came to be called "yellow rain." Analysis of these yellow spots on the leaf and stem was reported to show the presence of three lethal mycotoxins—poisons produced by fungi. Furthermore, the United States claimed that these mycotoxins did not occur naturally in Southeast Asia.

A State Department report in March 1982 declared, "the conclusion is inescapable that the toxins and other chemical warfare agents were developed in the Soviet Union." The Reagan Administration and its supporters in Congress began to routinely refer to "Soviet use of chemicals in Southeast Asia." Opposition to chemical arms declined in Congress, and increased funds were voted for their development.

An incident in the Soviet Union, first reported in

late 1979, also added to suspicions that the Soviets were violating the Biological Weapons Convention. In the city of Sverdlovsk (now called Yekaterinburg, its original name), hundreds of people died from anthrax. The Soviet government said that the anthrax outbreak was caused by contaminated meat. The Reagan Administration claimed that the anthrax spores had escaped after an accidental explosion at a secret biological warfare plant.

Some scientists were skeptical about the evidence used to support the charge of Soviet treaty violations. The epidemic could have arisen from natural causes; anthrax was a public health problem in the Soviet Union, and there had been past outbreaks in the Sverdlovsk region. Only in 1992, after the Soviet Union broke up, was the truth known. President Boris Yeltsin of Russia admitted that the anthrax breakout had been the result of an accident at a germ warfare plant.

The United State's case against the Soviets in Southeast Asia, however, eventually unraveled. Some journalists and scientists questioned the scant evidence. For example, the State Department based its case partly on a claim that yellow rain mycotoxins did not occur naturally in Southeast Asia. But experts on fungi said that the source of the mycotoxins, a fungus called *Fusarium,* could be found almost everywhere, including tropical Asia.

Some military experts wondered why mycotoxins would be chosen for chemical warfare. Whether the goal was to kill people, make them ill, or terrify them, other kinds of chemical weapons would have been more effective.

The main physical evidence was the yellow spots on one leaf and stem. Eventually, many more yellow rain samples were collected and analyzed by government laboratories in the United States and Great Britain. No mycotoxins were found. Government labs in France and Sweden had the same results. Could the initial test have been in error? This seemed more and more likely.

Nevertheless, the Reagan and later the Bush Administration, expressed no doubts about its evidence. In November 1982 the State Department sent to Congress and the United Nations a report entitled "Chemical Warfare in Southeast Asia and Afghanistan: An Update." At a news briefing about the report, a State Department official confirmed what several scientists had found: yellow rain samples contained pollen. This was not tiny wind-borne pollen, but larger grains of the sort that bees and other insects collect from flowers.

A government expert on poisons explained that the Soviets mixed mycotoxins, a solvent, and pollen. The solvent helped the toxins penetrate human skin. It was, she said, a "very clever mixture." A State Department spokesman also said, "I have no idea how the Soviets product this stuff. We've not been in their factory."

U.S. accusations that yellow rain was a communist weapon continued, but facts to the contrary kept popping up. Thomas Seeley, a biologist at Yale University who had studied bees in Southeast Asia, hearing a description of the yellow, pollen-filled spots on leaves, identified them as bee droppings.

In 1984 Thomas Seeley, Mathew Meselson (an early skeptic of the government's case) and a Thai bee expert— went into Thailand forests to learn more about yellow rain. They observed showers of honeybee feces that were mostly the outer shells of pollen grains. Bees digest the protein and fats within the pollen grain, then defecate the rest.

Bee experts came forward with more information about the mass "cleansing" flights of honeybees. In the tropics, according to a Canadian biologist, honeybees excrete waste as a way to cool their bodies. This helps keep the temperature within their colonies low enough so their larvae develop normally. Cleansing flights occur anywhere honeybees live, including Washington, D.C., where scientists found spots of yellow rain on cars parked near a honeybee colony. Chinese scientists had been aware of these harmless showers of bee feces since 1976. In fact, Chinese people were the first to use the term "yellow rain."

Yellow rain had been proved to bee feces. Physical evidence of chemical attacks from both Southeast Asia and Afghanistan was of dubious value. What, then, accounted for the claims of deaths, illness, and other details of chemical attacks? That evidence proved to be unreliable too.

An ancient Chinese saying comes to mind: "If you desire to find someone guilty, you need not fear a lack of evidence."

Pollen grains, shown magnified about 600 times, make up the bulk of honeybee feces, and of the alleged poison "yellow rain".

Government documents showed that U.S. interviewers failed to conduct impartial surveys. Hearsay was mixed with personal accounts. Also, many of the Laotian refugees were former members of an army supported by the U.S. Central Intelligence Agency (CIA). They knew in advance that the interviewers wanted to hear about chemical attacks. Refugees who were interviewed more carefully a second time admitted that they had not witnessed any chemical attacks or victims.

Nicolas Wade, a specialist in science affairs for *The New York Times*, wrote an editorial, "Rains of Error," in the newspaper's August 30, 1985 issue. "Yellow rain is bee excrement," he wrote, "a fact so preposterous and so embarrassing that even now the Administration cannot bring itself to accept it."

U.S. presidents have a wealth of scientific expertise at their disposal, including the National Academy of Sciences. In the case of yellow rain, however, the Reagan Administration could not be bothered with careful scientific investigation. For political reasons it rushed to claim the Soviet Union was conducting chemical warfare.

The Reagan Administration's scare tactics had the desired effect. In 1985 Congress authorized funds to produce binary chemical weapons. The first nerve gas artillery shells were produced in December 1987. The United States had ended its eighteen-year moratorium on producing chemical weapons.

5

Lessons From the Middle East

An arms control treaty can be a fragile thing. The treaty's strength is diminished when a nation flouts its rules and uses forbidden weapons. It is further weakened if other countries then do little to censure or punish the treaty-breaker. A treaty's strength can also be diminished when a nation makes false claims against another, using the arms control agreement as a political tool.

The Geneva Protocol and the Biological Weapons Convention were harmed by the Reagan Administration's unproven accusations of the Soviet Union. These arms control agreements were also hurt when the United States and other world powers virtually ignored outbreaks of chemical warfare in the Middle East.

The Middle East is home to a third of all countries that are capable of producing chemical weapons or are suspected of having them. These nations are Iran, Syria,

Israel, Libya, Ethiopia, and Egypt. Iraq also had chemical and biological arms until 1991, but had to destroy them to comply with the cease-fire agreement of the Persian Gulf War.

The most recent uses of chemical arms have also occurred in the Middle East. In the fall of 1962 Egypt entered a civil war in Yemen, battling Royalist forces that wanted to restore their leader to power. The Royalists controlled the mountains and other rugged terrain. They fought well, the war dragged on, and Egypt decided mustard attacks might settle matters quickly. In 1963 aircraft dropped mustard on several villages. Mostly civilian targets were chosen, perhaps because Royalist troops usually hid in caves. A British advisor to the Royalists said that he had seen and photographed "hideous sores and eruptions on the skin of children and animals who had been exposed to the gas." Egypt denied that any gas attacks had occurred, and only a few more were reported until the fall of 1966. Then mustard attacks resumed and increased in the spring and summer of 1967. Bombs containing mustard, and perhaps another chemical agent, fell on many villages, killing or injuring thousands of civilians. The Royalists showed no sign of weakening, however, and Egypt withdrew its forces from Yemen.

Despite abundant evidence that Egypt had used chemical weapons, no country made a formal protest to the United Nations. In 1967 Egypt had been crushed by Israel in the Six Day War. Rather than upset complex

political alliances with Middle Eastern nations, governments chose to ignore Egypt's gas warfare.

In September 1980 Iraq invaded Iran, and an eight-
year war began. As early as November 1980 Iran claimed
that Iraq had dropped chemical bombs. At first Iraq con-
quered some Iranian territory. Then the Iranian army
began to recover land that had been lost and capture
Iraqi soil. So the Iraqis stepped up their chemical attacks.
Iran formally complained to the United Nations in late
1983, and a U.N. fact-finding team was sent in 1984 to
inspect a battlefield site where chemical weapons were
reportedly used. The investigating team also visited Iranian hospitals and examined victims.

The U.N. scientists reported their findings in March
1984. They had found bomb fragments and unexploded
bombs, and the chemicals within these bombs proved to
be mustard and the nerve gas tabun. This was the first
time in history that a nerve gas was used in war.

The United Nations condemned this use of chemical
arms, as did the United States, but Iraq continued its
poison gas attacks through early 1988. (Iran reportedly
retaliated briefly in 1988.) Iraq was on the defensive,
outnumbered, and faced with massive Iranian "human
wave" attacks. Some mustard attacks seemed to be aimed
at contaminating the battlefield, creating a temporary
barrier that Iranian troops would not cross.

The Iran-Iraq war ended in August 1988. Iran
claimed nearly 50,000 casualties and several thousand

A United Nations investigating team inspects an unexploded Iraqi bomb in 1984. They found mustard and nerve gas in Iraqi bombs.

deaths from poison gas attacks. Aside from being scolded, however, Iraq was not punished for its use of illegal arms. Many governments were concerned about the militant power of Islamic Iran. Some, including the United States, were officially neutral but wanted Iraq and its leader, Saddam Hussein, to remain strong. No economic sanctions were imposed on Iraq, although the United States and several other nations banned the export to Iraq and Iran of certain chemicals that can be used to make chemical weapons. This made it more difficult but not impossible for Iraq to replenish its stocks of chemical arms.

In March 1988 Iraq attacked its own citizens with mustard and nerve gas. A Kurdish rebellion was put down after mustard caused a reported 5,000 deaths in the Iraqi town of Halabja. Earlier, in 1987, Libya reportedly used chemical arms in a war with its neighbor Chad. Neither Libya nor Iraq suffered any harm from breaking the moral barriers of international law. They showed other Third World nations that these laws could be defied without punishment.

By the time Iraq invaded Kuwait in 1990, it had rebuilt its supplies and had the largest and most sophisticated chemical weapons program in the Third World. It could deliver chemical weapons from aircraft and with artillery fire and rockets. Iraq was also believed to have biological weapons. As the United States and its allies prepared for the 1990–1991 Persian Gulf War, the

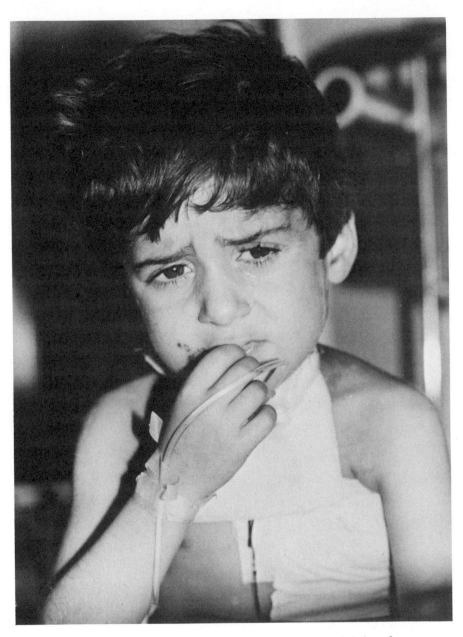

Bandages cover blisters caused by mustard on a Kurdish boy from the town of Halabja in Iraq.

threat of both poison gases and germ warfare was a cause of concern.

Troops were vaccinated against anthrax. Masks and protective clothing also defended soldiers against both biological and chemical arms. The gas masks had two kinds of filters. One removed particles, including dangerous microorganisms. The other, made of activated charcoal, adsorbed molecules of chemical gas. (In *ad*sorption, molecules stick to the charcoal's surface, and are not taken in, as when water is *ab*sorbed by a sponge.)

Troops also wore jackets and pants of two layers, with charcoal foam in the inner layer to trap toxic gases. They wore rubber gloves and overboots as well. In addition, they carried a package of medicated towelettes in case their skin was exposed to mustard gas or other blistering agents. And they also were given injectors that would give them a quick antidote against nerve gas.

Each soldier carried adhesive-backed paper strips that could be stuck on their protective suits, and which turned red when touched by poisonous chemicals. Troop units also had air sampling devices and alarms to warn of chemical attack. In addition, U.S. forces had sixty German-built Fox chemical detection vehicles. These lightly-armored, fast-moving vehicles were laboratories on wheels. They were equipped with sensors and a computer for detecting chemical agents in the air. The Foxes were expected to roam front lines and warn ground forces away from areas contaminated by chemicals.

There was great concern about the ability of Allied troops to function if a chemical attack forced them to wear their cumbersome protective clothing and gear. Daytime temperatures can reach 49°C (120°F) in the Arabian desert. The U.S. Army had special air-conditioned tents prepared to help soldiers cope with this problem.

Allied forces were well-protected, but their commanders worried about the combat effectiveness of troops facing chemical attack. Gas masks impair vision and gloves impair the dexterity of fingers. Simple tasks, like digging a foxhole, and complicated ones, like rearming a helicopter, would take longer on a chemical battlefield. According to U.S. Army studies, this "operational degradation" could range from 30 to 50 percent.

All of this concern and preparation proved to be unnecessary. Despite repeated threats by President Saddam Hussein, Iraq never unleashed its arsenal of chemical weapons.

Although Iraqi gas masks and antidotes were left behind by retreating troops, Iraqi prisoners said that most of their units had inadequate protection against chemical attack. Allied aircraft had also dropped leaflets warning Iraqi commanders they would be held responsible if they used chemical weapons. Wind patterns and heavy rains may also have discouraged use of these weapons. So, too, did the swift success of Allied forces.

U.S. soldiers maintain a desert outpost, dressed in gear designed to protect them from chemical and biological weapons.

The Fox vehicle is a mobile laboratory for detecting and analyzing chemical weapons.

Preparing for the 1991 Persian Gulf War, allied troops wore gas masks and protective clothing. Such gear can be a handicap in a hot desert environment.

The Scud missiles Iraq launched toward Israel and Saudi Arabia were one of the most dramatic elements of the war. Television viewers all over the world saw images of Israeli citizens wearing gas masks and taking shelter in sealed rooms. However, the missiles contained conventional explosives, not poison gases. Why? One explanation was that Iraq had not developed the needed technology, including a fuse that would cause a missile to explode and release a gas cloud before striking the ground. Saddam Hussein may have feared alienating his Palestinian supporters in Israel. He certainly also had reason to fear chemical retaliation from the United States and its allies, or from Israel itself.

Soon after the war's end, Iraq reportedly used mustard against its own rebellious people who tried to overthrow Saddam Hussein. A threat of U.S. air strikes stopped this tactic. Required by the United Nations to destroy its nuclear, chemical, and biological weapons, Iraq in April 1991 released its tally of chemical arms. It admitted to having nearly 10,000 nerve gas warheads, more than 1,000 tons of nerve and mustard gas, nearly 1,500 chemical bombs and shells, and 30 Scud missiles armed with chemical warheads.

Later in 1991, however, U.N. inspectors discovered that Iraq had many more chemical weapons than it had declared. This was just one of several instances of Iraqi resistance to complying with the terms of the U.N. cease-fire agreement.

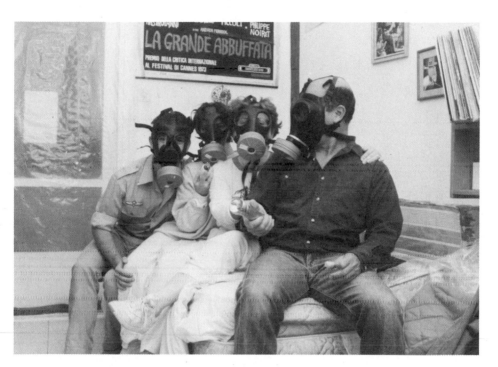

Warned of Scud missile attacks during the Persian Gulf War, Israelis donned gas masks and took shelter in sealed rooms.

These Iraqi bombs, destroyed by the United Nations inspectors, had been equipped to carry chemical weapons.

Like World War II, the Persian Gulf War ended with no chemical weapons used, even though both sides had such weapons. In the Middle East and elsewhere, there is a pattern in the history of chemical and biological warfare. Fear of retaliation, and knowing that one's enemy is well-defended against chemical attack, discourage a nation from using its chemical arms.

Throughout history, the victims of chemical and biological attacks have been troops or civilians who initially have no protection. Thus, chemical and biological arms may be the cruelest of all weapons.

This pattern will no doubt continue as long as there are chemical and biological arsenals. The most powerful nations will not need to use their stocks, but Third World countries, acting aggressively or out of desperation, will be tempted to unleash their cruel weapons.

6

New, Improved
Ways to Kill

The 1972 Biological Weapons Convention was a remarkable achievement. It was the first arms control
treaty calling for the destruction of an entire class of
weapons. Furthermore, nations that signed it agreed
never in any circumstances to develop, produce, stockpile, or otherwise acquire or retain microbes or other
biological agents, or toxins, as well as weapons, equipment, or ways of delivering such agents or toxins for
hostile purposes.

More than 100 nations have agreed to these terms,
partly because biological weapons seem terrible and inhumane, but also because military experts don't favor
them. "Germ" weapons are dangerous to handle, difficult
to spread effectively, and—once released—impossible to
control.

This is as true today as it was in the early 1970s.

However, interest in biological weapons has grown. The possibility of creating more deadly and manageable biological weapons now exists. So the United States, which has agreed to the terms of the Biological Weapons Convention, now argues that it must study ways of detecting such weapons and defending people against them.

The possibility of creating new varieties of biological weapons arose in the early 1970s, when scientists discovered how to combine the genetic materials of two organisms. They "spliced" a gene from one organism into the genetic material (DNA) of another. This created a new life form, with characteristics of both organisms. They also developed ways of mass producing these new life forms.

This new technology—called biotechnology or genetic engineering—has already been used to cheaply mass-produce insulin and vaccines that were once in short supply. In agriculture, progress has been made in improving crop yields and plant resistance to pests. Genetic engineering has enormous potential for good.

It also has great potential for harm, though not as great as some journalists and politicians have claimed. In 1984, for example, a reporter for *The Wall Street Journal* claimed that "Soviet scientists were attempting to recombine the venom-producing genes from cobra snakes with ordinary viruses and bacteria: such an organism would infect the body and surreptitiously produce paralytic cobra neurotoxin." In other words, a person would get the effects of a deadly cobra bite from a simple microorganism.

Experts say that this imagined threat is farfetched, given the present nature of genetic engineering. Its dangers are not likely to come from creating brand-new diseases, but from modifying existing ones so that it will be easier to wage germ warfare. For example, genetic engineering could alter a deadly but rare disease organism into one that could be cheaply mass-produced. This is just one way in which genetic engineering could produce weapons of war. Others include:

- improving the ability of microorganisms to survive after being sprayed from ships or aircraft, or released from bombs or missiles.
- toughening viruses or other germs so that they can overcome the natural resistance of people, and even of troops that have been vaccinated against the germs. (This would be achieved by altering the antigens on the outer surface of a virus, a change that would also make the disease agent harder to detect and identify.)
- increasing the deadliness of a disease, for example, by changing the anthrax bacterium so that it produces a stronger toxin.
- speeding up the action of a disease organism, so that it causes illness within hours rather than days.

- changing a common, relatively harmless bacterium into one that produces toxins.
- applying some of these kinds of changes to microbes that harm livestock or crop plants, so that a nation's food supply and economy could be damaged.

Research on genetic engineering may lead to these changes, but only with a great investment of money and time. In the United States that investment began in the early 1980s, when the Department of Defense began awarding contracts for biotechnology research.

The Reagan Administration promoted this change by claiming that the Soviet Union was engaged in illegal work on biological weapons. In 1984 Secretary of Defense Caspar Weinberger said:

> We continue to obtain new evidence that the Soviet Union has maintained its offensive biological warfare program and that it is exploring genetic engineering to expand their program's scope. Consequently, it is essential and urgent that we develop and field adequate biological and toxin protection.

Some people wondered whether the evidence mentioned was any more reliable than that which "proved" that bee feces was a Soviet-made chemical weapon. Nevertheless, Congress voted increased funds for research on genetic engineering by the Department of Defense. In 1980 there were no funds for this kind of research, but by the late 1980s well over $100 million was spent each year. By 1988 the number of U.S. military research projects on genetic engineering had grown to ninety-nine. (They are briefly described in an appendix of *Preventing a Biological Arms Race,* listed in the Further Reading section of this book.)

According to the Department of Defense, very little of this research is secret and all of it is defensive—as required by the Biological Weapons Convention. A number of scientists have observed, however, that the line between defensive and offensive research is unclear and easily crossed.

To develop defenses against biological weapons, studies have included methods of detecting disease agents as well as countermeasures, such as protective clothing and vaccines. They have also included basic research on potential disease agents and on ways in which an enemy might try to deliver them. All of these studies could yield practical information for waging biological war. (In World War II, Japan's secret germ-warfare research was officially described as work on vaccines and ways to purify water.)

The year 1985 marked a quick thaw and end of the Cold War and friendlier relations between the United States and the Soviet Union. In 1987 the Soviets made important concessions that removed obstacles to a treaty outlawing chemical arms (the Chemical Weapons Convention). However, American interest in biological weapons research remained high. No longer able to blame the Soviets, the U.S. government expressed growing concern about the spread of such weapons to Third World nations and to terrorist groups.

Terrorists or guerrilla army units could use biological weapons to contaminate water supplies, kill crops and livestock, and cause local epidemics. There have already been charges that such weapons have been used covertly by enemy agents. In 1971, for example, Cuba claimed that agents of the CIA had released several diseases. One was African swine fever virus, which broke out in two far-apart sites. In order to halt the epidemic, a half million pigs were slaughtered. Cuba also blamed the CIA for outbreaks of dengue fever, which made 350,000 people ill, and diseases that harmed tobacco and sugar cane crops.

Whether or not these charges were true, the CIA is better able to attack in this way than a terrorist or guerrilla group. Biological weapons are relatively cheap, but require more expertise to produce than most chemical or conventional weapons, such as bombs. Terrorists can make sophisticated bombs, but are not likely to splice genes and create new disease microbes. In fact, they would be more likely to attempt theft of biological weapons than to make them.

In 1989 Jonathan King, molecular biologist at the Massachusetts Institute of Technology said, "The danger from terrorists is not their development of biological weapons, but rather a raid" on a facility where they are studied. "Therefore," he concluded, "protection from

Biological weapons can harm people directly, or indirectly, by damaging their food supplies or cash crops, such as sugar cane.

terrorism lies in the direction of strengthening the treaty and prohibiting the establishment of biological research for military purposes."

Genetic engineering has raised fears, and it does open opportunities to wage more effective germ warfare. However, scientists who are well-informed about biotechnology say that these hazards have been exaggerated, and that drawbacks remain. Old or new, biological weapons would still be more difficult to use, with less predictable results, than chemical or conventional arms. More important, they would have the potential of raging out of control.

Unlike other weapons, germs can reproduce. A biological weapon could sweep through a population, then keep going, infecting the troops and perhaps the civilians of the nation that launched it.

In this way, germ warfare—especially with microbes "improved" by genetic engineering—is a global threat. Rather than trying to develop defenses, the wise course is to make a greater effort to discourage research on biological weapons, at home and abroad.

Controlling the Cruelest Weapons

By 1990 more than 1,000 U.S. scientists had signed a statement that opposed the use of science for the development of chemical and biological weapons. The statement noted the growing military interest in such arms, then concluded:

> We are concerned that this may lead to another arms race. We believe that biomedical research should support rather than threaten life. Therefore, we pledge not to engage knowingly in research and teaching that will further the development of chemical and biological warfare agents.

Many scientists, members of Congress, and citizens had become alarmed about military research on these weapons. That research continued into the administration of President George Bush, who took office in 1989. Congress launched an inquiry into the safety of U.S. biological and chemical studies. In 1990 Congress tried but failed to establish a law that would impose sanctions on companies and governments that sold materials or helped in other ways to produce chemical or biological weapons.

Dramatic change in global politics offered some hope that the dangers of these weapons would finally be faced, and reduced. New policies of the Soviet Union opened the way for completion of the Chemical Weapons Convention. In the late 1980s the Soviet Union stopped producing chemical arms and advocated wide-ranging inspection of chemical production and storage places. Early in 1989 the Soviet Union announced that it would start destroying its stocks of chemical weapons. Two years later the Soviet Union and the United States agreed on a plan to slash their arsenals of poison gas.

Most of each country's stocks of poison gas were to be destroyed by the end of the century, leaving each nation with 5,000 tons in the year 2002. Unfortunately, getting rid of chemical weapons is difficult and costly. A Soviet official said, "To destroy chemical weapons is more expensive than to make them."

It could cost $20 billion to get rid of the Soviet chemical arsenal. Moreover, the Soviet Union's only facility for the task was shut down as a result of protests from environmentalists. The U.S. Army proposed burning up to *sixty million* pounds of its mustard and nerve agents in nine incinerators. This plan, too, drew criticism from some environmentalists and people living near the proposed incinerator sites.

Chemical disarmament by two major world powers was a hopeful sign, but only a tiny step. An arms control conference, held in Paris in 1989, resulted in 149 countries calling for "a global and comprehensive and effectively verifiable" chemical weapons treaty to be reached at an early date. Behind these noble words, however, remained major obstacles to such a treaty. Concerned about Israel's nuclear weapons, Arab nations tried to link chemical disarmament to nuclear disarmament.

Since the United States was still producing binary chemical weapons, and France declared it also planned to do so, Egypt and other Arab countries wondered why they shouldn't seek such arms. As an Egyptian diplomat put it, referring to the policies of the United States, "How can I ask my child to stop smoking if I continue to smoke myself?"

At the 1989 chemical arms control conference, the United States opposed efforts to censure Iraq and Libya for their chemical attacks on neighbors. (This stance was in inducement for these countries to attend, which they did.) A year later intelligence reports revealed that Libya had resumed making chemical weapons. These events underscored the need for international agreement on getting tough with those who use such weapons and on

Chemical arms are stored in dozens of these shelters in Utah. Getting rid of them safely is more costly than making them.

restricting the sale of materials that can be used to make chemical arms.

Many of the raw materials used to make chemical arms are fairly harmless and common until processed. Thiodigylcol, for example, has many uses. It is used to make ink for ballpoint pens and in finishing textiles. When it is mixed with hydrochloric acid, however, the product is mustard.

Thiodigylcol is one of nine chemicals closely linked to manufacture of chemical weapons. Trade in these nine chemicals needs to be carefully controlled. About fifty other chemicals are often used in producing chemical arms, so their sale should be monitored too. For trade restrictions to work, however, all nations that export chemicals must cooperate.

During the 1980s Iraq acquired the chemicals and equipment it needed to make chemical weapons from companies in West Germany, France, Belgium, and Italy. A group of western nations, including the United States, tightened their export rules, agreeing to closely monitor and restrict sales of chemicals and equipment needed for making poison gases. As a result, Iraq, Iran, and other Middle Eastern nations began to obtain needed chemicals from India. The western nations pressed India to stop such trade. Instead, India called for a worldwide ban on chemical weapons.

In 1992 this ban was agreed to by negotiators from thirty-eight nations. They completed a landmark

Johnson Island, an atoll about 750 miles southwest of Hawaii, is the site of a chemical weapons incinerator where the U.S. Army plans to dispose of nerve gases.

agreement —the Chemical Weapons Convention—that in early 1993 was signed by many nations in Paris, France.

The treaty would go into force two years after it was opened for signing, or six months after sixty-five nations had both signed and ratified it, whichever is later. This delay was established to allow time to set up a new international agency that would make far-reaching inspections of chemical plants around the world.

This treaty verification system had possible loopholes. Surprise inspections were ruled out; a country would have five day's notice. Some experts on chemical arms believe that this is not enough time for a country to conceal chemical arms-making activity. Others point out that many of these weapons can be made in small plants, including the sort that make pesticides, drugs, and even a component of ink for ballpoint pens. If warned of an inspection, a small-scale illegal arms-making operation could be hidden or dismantled in a few hours.

In negotiations the inspection system had been weakened at the insistence of the United States, as the Bush Administration heeded the concern of chemical companies. They were worried that inspectors might learn trade secrets.

Nevertheless, the Chemical Weapons Convention was a major step toward eliminating these weapons from the world. It banned the production, stockpiling, and use of chemical arms, and called for destruction of all existing stocks by the year 2005. The United States

Can the world community of nations reduce the threat of chemical and biological warfare?

expected to get rid of its chemical arms by the year 2000, and in 1992 was working with Russia to develop a plan for destroying the chemical weapons of the former Soviet Union.

One great question loomed: Which nations would sign the treaty and agree with its terms? Libya, Syria, Egypt, and several other nations believed to possess chemical weapons were not expected to sign at first. Perhaps they will do so eventually, now that the world's community of nations has made it clear that possessing chemical arms is illegal. For the ban on chemical arms to be successful, the world's nations might have to impose tough sanctions—political, economic, and perhaps military—against countries that wage either chemical or biological warfare.

The 1990s began with great promise in arms control, as the United States and the Soviet Union agreed to reduce their nuclear arsenals. The breakup of the Soviet Union then hastened the process of arms reduction. Now, a landmark treaty banning chemical arms offers new hope that the world's nations will take the necessary steps to avoid an arms race with humankind's cruelest weapons.

The threat of chemical and biological warfare continues today.

Chemical and Biological Arms

Listed on the next three pages are all chemical and biological weapons that have been used in war, and many others that have been studied for that purpose. More complete lists appear in the appendices of *Gene Wars* and *Preventing a Biological Arms Race* (see Further Reading, page 97).

Chemical Weapons

Tear gases: CAP (CN), CS, and Adamsite (DM). Also called harassing agents, irritant agents, or incapacitants, these substances act rapidly and can cause short-term flow of tears, itching or burning feeling in skin, coughing, sneezing, and vomiting.

Choking gases: Chlorine, Phosgene, and Chloropicrin. Once inhaled, these gases inflame lung tissues, causing fluids to build up, leading to bronchitis, pneumonia, and sometimes death, as the victim drowns from within.

Blistering agents: Mustards (Sulfur or Nitrogen) and Lewisite. Also called vesicants, blistering agents attack the skin and eyes, causing burns, blisters, and blindness that can last a week or more. Inhaled high concentrations can be lethal.

Blood agents: Hydrogen cyanide and Cyanogen chloride. Blood agents act by destroying an enzyme in red blood cells needed for oxygen to be released to body tissues. Low doses cause headache, nausea, and fatigue. High doses cause rapid breathing, paralysis, and convulsions.

Nerve agents: Tabun, Sarin, Soman, and VX. Nerve agents act by breaking down an enzyme needed where nerves relay signals to muscles. Without the enzyme, muscles contract wildly. Low doses cause sweating and tremors. High doses cause breathing difficulty, nausea, cramps, twitching, involuntary defecation, staggering, coma, and convulsion. An inhaled large dose can cause death in a few minutes.

Possible Biological Weapons

Diseases caused by viruses:

Influenza	Lassa fever
Dengue fever	Rift Valley fever
Equine encephalitis	Smallpox
Ebola fever	Yellow fever

Diseases caused by bacteria:

Anthrax	Plague
Cholera	Tetanus
Dysentery	Tularemia
Glanders	Typhoid
Legionnaires' Disease	

Disease caused by rickettsiae:

Q-fever

Natural toxins and their sources:

Toxin	Source
Aflatoxin	fungus
Batrachotoxin	Columbian Frog
Botulin	bacterium
Cobrotoxin	Chinese cobra
Crotoxin	South American rattlesnake
Coral toxins	corals
Ricin	Castor Bean plant
Saxitoxin	shellfish
Sea Wasp toxin	jellyfish
Staphyloccus	bacterium
Tetanus toxin	bacterium

The Chemical Weapons Convention*

Excerpted from the *Fact Sheet* of July 23, 1992, published by the United States Arms Control and Disarmament Agency, Washington, D.C.:

The Chemical Weapons Convention, when concluded, would ban the production, acquisition, stockpiling, and use of chemical weapons.

In it each State Party undertakes never, under any circumstances, to:

- develop, produce, otherwise acquire, stockpile or retain chemical weapons, or transfer, directly or indirectly, chemical weapons to anyone;
- use chemical weapons;
- engage in any military preparations to use chemical weapons; and
- assist, encourage or induce, in any way, anyone to engage in any activity prohibited to a State Party under this Convention.

---

* At the time of publication of this book, the exact text from the Chemical Weapons Convention was unavailable. The following excerpts present some of the goals and ideas included in that text.

In addition each State Party undertakes, all in accordance with the provisions of the Convention to:

- destroy the chemical weapons it owns or possesses or that are located in any place under its jurisdiction or control;
- destroy all chemical weapons it abandoned on the territory of another State Party; and
- destroy any chemical weapons production facilities it owns or possesses or that are located in any place under its jurisdiction or control.

Finally, each State Party undertakes not to use riot control agents as a method of warfare.

The Chemical Weapons Convention provides for both routine and challenge inspections to assist in the verification of compliance with the Convention.

Routine Inspections of declared facilities which are both intrusive and conducted on short notice are mandated by the Convention. "Declared facilities" include all government chemical weapons facilities as well as civilian chemical facilities that use certain chemicals which could be used or converted to make chemical weapons. These facilities must be identified to an international body when the Treaty enters into force.

Challenge Inspections may be conducted at any facility where a Party suspects illegal activities. These inspections will be on short demand and, under the principles of managed access, will allow the inspectors to visit the site and investigate to determine whether or not banned activities are taking place. Any State Party can issue a challenge inspection. The Inspections will be conducted by the International Technical Secretariat and the inspectors will render a report of their inspection findings to the Executive Council.

Excerpted from the *Official Text* of the Address by Ambassador Ronald F. Lehman II, Director, United States Arms Control and Disarmament Agency, before the Conference on Disarmament Plenary Meeting, Geneva, Switzerland, of September 3, 1992:

. . . For the first time on a multilateral level, states have agreed to a complete prohibition of an entire category of weapons together with appropriate enforcement machinery. The objective of the Chemicals Weapons Convention is not simply to curb the spread of chemical weapons or to preserve the status quo; rather it is to eliminate an entire type of weapon, weapons that exist in large quantities and have been used in combat.

This prohibition will be absolute. All activities for offensive chemical weapons purposes will be banned, not just the use of such weapons. All existing chemical weapons will be destroyed, not just some of them. All areas of the world will be protected, not just a specific region or a few states.

. . . The unprecedented scope of the convention requires unprecedented verification measures. The convention provides for declaration and inspection of chemical weapons and chemical weapons production facilities, for continued inspection until they are destroyed, and for inspection of destruction. Inspectors can be present continuously during the chemical weapons destruction process.

Verification requirements for the convention are also driven by the complex relationship between chemical activities that will be prohibited and those that will not. Both developed and developing societies depend on a wide variety of chemical activities. Unfortunately, many common industrial chemicals, and the facilities that produce them, can be misused for chemical weapons purposes. The task of the negotiators has been to develop measures that will be effective in verifying compliance, but not unduly interfere with legitimate industrial activities. The convention therefore provides for a hierarchy of measures in which the level of monitoring is based on the level of risk. The greater the risk, the more intrusive the monitoring. As a result, verification will focus on those few activities that pose the greatest risk. Where permitted activities pose less risk, other less stringent measures will be applied that will, nonetheless, help reduce the potential for circumvention of the system.

A safety net for the verification system is provided by

challenge inspection provisions. These go well beyond analogous measures in other recent agreements. At the same time, the legitimate concerns of the inspected state party are well-protected. Another innovation in the verification system is the concept of coordinating bilateral and multilateral verification efforts. This will help to reduce the direct costs of implementing the convention without reducing the level of assurance provided to the parties.

To oversee the operation of the convention, in particular the implementation of its verification provisions, an important new international organization will be created. The verification responsibilities of this organization—and thus the demands placed on it—go much further than those borne by the International Atomic Energy Agency and other existing bodies under normal circumstances.

This combination of strict verification of weapons production facilities and extensive monitoring of commercial industrial activities is unique to the Chemical Weapons Convention. It is an imaginative and practical solution to a unique problem.

In addition to the scope and the verification system, the convention is unprecedented in the assurances given to developing countries. Article X provides for assistance to a state attacked or simply threatened with chemical weapons. Emergency assistance shall be provided immediately.

Security assurances in Article X are supplemented by economic assurances in Article XI. These provisions mean that the convention will encourage the development of chemical industry, rather than hamper it. At the same time, states retain their sovereign right to control the export of chemicals and equipment from their territory to promote important national security and foreign policy goals. I would note that members of the Australia Group have given assurances that they will review their chemical weapons-related controls with a view to removing them on exports to states parties that are in full compliance with the convention. I would also note that the convention imposes restrictions on trade with non-states parties. This is an important step to encourage universal adherence to the convention.

Finally, with respect to costs, we believe that from the very beginning close attention must be paid to the financial aspects of implementing the convention's provisions. We are sensitive to the economic burdens that already weigh heavily on states, particularly for those currently experiencing difficult economic conditions. We are prepared to work closely with others, during the preparatory period and after the convention enters into force, to help keep costs down, consistent with the needs for effective implementation of the convention's provisions. . . .

Further Reading

Books or other sources marked with an asterisk (*) were especially useful in research for this book.

Berstein, Barton. "The Birth of the U.S. Biological-Warfare Program." *Scientific American,* June 1987, pp. 116–121.

Brown, Frederick. *Chemical Warfare: A Study in Restraints.* Princeton, N.J.: Princeton University Press, 1968.

Cecil, Paul. *Herbicidal Warfare: The RANCH HAND Project in Vietnam.* New York: Praeger, 1986.

*Cole, Leonard. *Clouds of Secrecy: The Army's Germ Warfare Tests Over Populated Areas.* Totowa, N.J.: Rowman & Littlefield, 1988.

Flowerree, Charles, and Gordon Burck. *International Handbook on Chemical Weapons Proliferation.* Westport, Conn.: Greenwood Press, 1991.

Geissler, Erhard, ed. *Biological and Toxin Weapons Today.* New York: Oxford University Press, 1986.

Haber, Ludwig. *The Poisonous Cloud: Chemical Warfare in the First World War.* New York: Oxford University Press, 1986.

King, Jonathan. "The Threat of Biological Weapons." *Technology Review,* May-June 1982, pp. 10–11.

Marshall, Eliot. "Iraq's Chemical Warfare: Case Proved." *Science,* April 13, 1984, pp. 130–132.

*Meselson, Matthew. "The Myth of Chemical Superweapons." *Bulletin of the Atomic Scientists,* April 1991, pp. 12–15.

Montross, Lynn. *War Through the Ages.* New York: Harper, 1960.

O'Connell, Robert. *Of Arms and Men: A History of War, Weapons, and Aggression.* New York: Oxford University Press, 1989.

*Piller, Charles, and Keith Yamamoto. Gene Wars: Military Control Over the New Genetic Technologies. New York: William Morrow, 1988. (The appendices of this book include tables of biological and chemical weapons, and text of the treaties aimed at controlling them.)

*Robinson, Julian, J. Guillemin, and M. Meselson. "Yellow Rain: the Story Collapses." Foreign Policy, Fall 1987, pp. 100–117. (An updated version of this article appears on pages 220–235 of *Preventing a Biological Arms Race,* cited below.)

Rose, Steven. "Biotechnology at War." *New Scientist,* March 19, 1987, pp. 33–37.

*Seeley, Thomas, et al. "Yellow Rain." *Scientific American,* September 1985, pp. 128–137.

*Spiers, Edward. *Chemical Weaponry: A Continuing Challenge.* New York: St. Martin's Press, 1989.

United Nations General Assembly. *Report of the Secretary-General on Chemical and Bacteriological (Biological) Weapons and the Effects of Their Possible Use.* New York: United Nations, 1969.

Warry, John. *Warfare in the Classical World.* New York: St. Martin's Press, 1980.

*Whiteside, Thomas. "The Yellow-Rain Complex." *The New Yorker,* February 11, 1991, pp. 38–67, and February 18, 1991, pp. 44–68.

*Wright, Susan. "The Buildup That Was." *Bulletin of the Atomic Scientists,* January-February 1989, pp. 52–56.

*Wright, Susan. "New Designs for Biological Weapons." *Bulletin of the Atomic Scientists,* January-February 1987, pp. 43–46.

*Wright, Susan, ed. *Preventing a Biological Arms Race.* Cambridge, Mass.: MIT Press, 1990. (Composed of sixteen chapters by experts on the science, technology, history, and law of biological weapons. This book also includes descriptions of biological, chemical, and toxin warfare agents as well as texts of treaties in its appendices.)

Index

Syracuse (Greece), 13
Syria, 53, 85

T

tabun, 26, 55
Tartars, 14, 16
tear gases, 17, 24, 31, 38, 42
terrorists, 74, 76
Thailand, 45, 50
thiodigylcol, 81
toxins, 29, 44, 47, 69, 71, 72
typhus, 28

U

undulant fever, 29
United Nations, 10, 24, 41, 42,
    49, 54, 55, 64
United States, 12, 17, 25, 26,
    28, 29, 31, 32, 34,
    37–52, 55, 57, 59, 64,
    70, 72–74, 77, 79, 81,
    83, 85
U.S. Army, 34, 36, 45, 78
U.S. Congress, 37, 41, 47, 49,
    52, 72, 77–78
U.S. Department of Defense,
    44, 72, 73
U.S. Senate, 34
U.S. State Department, 45, 47,
    48, 49

V

Viet Cong, 38, 39
Vietnam. *See* South Vietnam.
viruses, 14, 70, 71, 74
VX nerve gas, 36

W

Wade, Nicolas, 52
Wall Street Journal, The, 70–71
Webster, William, 12
Weinberger, Caspar, 72
whooping cough, 32, 34
World War I, 17–24, 28
World War II, 26, 29, 67, 73

Y

yellow fever, 28, 32
"yellow rain," 47, 48–52
Yeltsin, Boris, 48
Yemen, 54
Ypres, Belgium, 17, 20

About the Author

Laurence Pringle is the author of many outstanding nonfiction books for young people. His title *Restoring Our Earth* (Enslow) was chosen as best book of the year by both the National Science Teachers Association and the National Council for the Social Studies. In 1983 he received the Eva L. Gordon Award of the American Nature Study Society. Mr. Pringle earned degrees in wildlife conservation from Cornell University and the University of Massachusetts.